Speed Reading

*The Definitive Guide for Learning
How to Read a Book a Day*

By: Lawrence Franz

© **Copyright 2018 - All rights reserved.**

The contents of this book may not be reproduced, duplicated or transmitted without direct written permission from the author.

Under no circumstances will any legal responsibility or blame be held against the publisher for any reparation, damages, or monetary loss due to the information herein, either directly or indirectly.

Legal Notice:

You cannot amend, distribute, sell, use, quote or paraphrase any part of the content within this book without the consent of the author.

Disclaimer Notice:

Please note the information contained within this document is for educational and entertainment purposes only. No warranties of any kind are expressed or implied. Readers acknowledge that the author is not engaging in the rendering of legal, financial, medical or professional advice. Please consult a licensed professional before attempting any techniques outlined in this book.

By reading this document, the reader agrees that under no circumstances are the author responsible for any losses, direct or indirect, which are incurred as a result of the use of information contained within this document, including, but not limited to, —errors, omissions, or inaccuracies.

Table of Contents

Introduction 5

Chapter 1: The True Nature of Speed Reading 7

Chapter 2: Assessing Your Reading Habits 15

Chapter 3: Breaking Bad Reading Habits 25

Chapter 4: Creating Good Reading Habits 36

Chapter 5: Proven Speed Reading Techniques 46

Chapter 6: Creating Your Daily Reading Practice 57

Chapter 7: Some Simple Exercises 70

Conclusion 80

Introduction

Speed reading is a skill that has become highly sought after in recent years. With time becoming an increasingly rare commodity, many people find that they can't read as much as they want to or as much as they were once able to. Furthermore, many work places require that a person becomes familiar with vast quantities of information in a very short amount of time, far faster than conventional reading speeds would allow for. It is for these reasons, as well as many others that more and more people are pursuing the skill set of speed reading. This book will present the various techniques of speed reading, which will teach you how to read more quickly, efficiently and effectively. Not only will these techniques increase your reading speed but they will also increase your ability to obtain and retain information with greater speed and ease.

Furthermore, they will teach you how to identify and ignore the vast amounts of fluff and filler that make up the majority of any written material. By the time you finish reading this book, you will be able to improve your reading abilities so that you can read as much as a book a day. In fact, this will be the last book you read the wrong way ever again!

Chapter 1: The True Nature of Speed Reading

like an expert. This is the true nature of speed reading and the benefits it offers. In order to get the best results from your efforts, it is important to first understand the true nature of speed reading. Most people think of speed reading as the ability to read words at a faster rate. While this is a part of the speed reading process it is not the entirety, nor is it even the most important part. Instead, speed reading is about being able to obtain information contained within a written document at a faster rate. This can be done in several different ways, each focusing on different elements of how to read written material. The bottom line is that speed reading is intended to teach you to know what to read as well as what to ignore. By being able to identify and skip over all irrelevant content you can focus your attention on the words that contain vital information. This allows you to obtain information from any written document in a fraction of the time that it takes most other people. While it may seem as though you are able to read with superhuman speed, the fact is that you simply know how to read

What speed reading isn't

What most people expect to be able to do once they acquire the skill of speed reading is to be able to read upwards of a thousand words per minute, allowing them to breeze through a book like an android. Unfortunately, that goal is simply impossible. One reason for this is that it is physiologically unlikely that you will be able to train your eyes to perceive more than about 500 words per minute. Anything more will significantly reduce your ability to identify the words you see, let alone retain the information they contain. Therefore, while speed reading techniques can significantly increase your reading speed, they can't transform your reading beyond a certain fixed point. That said, the average reading speed is around 200 words per minute, so if you were to increase to the 500 word per minute range, you would reduce the amount of time it takes to read a book by over half.

Another thing that speed reading isn't is a magic wand. You won't find a secret formula or strategy that allows you to suddenly read a text in half the time it would ordinarily take you. Instead, speed reading is a skill that you develop over time with continuous commitment and effort. In a way, it's a bit like weight training. Just as you wouldn't expect to go to the gym for a few sessions and walk out ready for the Iron Man competition, so too, don't expect to achieve maximum speed reading results overnight. While you will be able to see measurable improvement right away, the overall goal will take time to achieve. Only when a person commits to training themselves on a daily basis will they break through the barriers that keep them from reaching their full potential. Therefore, don't expect this to be quick and easy. It will take time and effort, but the results will be more than worth it.

Understanding how things are written

In order to understand how speed reading works you must first understand how things are actually written. More often than not a text will contain far more words than it actually needs to. This isn't for any sinister reason, such as someone trying to hide information within the countless extra words. Instead, it's for better presentation. The truth is that you can express a thought in as little as two or three words, depending on the situation. If you suddenly found yourself hungry, you could simply say "feed me now." Those three words would successfully convey the pertinent information. Unfortunately, they would do so in a way that seemed rude and demanding. Subsequently, you will probably express your feelings of hunger by saying something more along the lines of "I'm feeling pretty hungry all of a sudden. How about we get something to eat?" This sentence is far more conversational and polite, and will doubtlessly be better received. However, it is also five times as long as the original statement, meaning that you took five times the number of words than actually needed in order to get your point across.

Writing does the very same thing. While it's true that you could write a document in such a way as to only use as many words as necessary in order to convey information, such a document would be disjointed, hard to read and fairly boring. In fact, it would probably be like trying to read a phone book. As a result, the average document is written in a way that makes reading it more enjoyable and engaging. Unfortunately, this means that the average document uses far more words than needed in order to convey the information it contains. Speed reading recognizes this fact and addresses it by training the individual to look for information rather than at all of the words a document possesses. Once you learn to look beyond the words, you will be able to obtain the information you need without having to labor through each and every written word in the process. Therefore, rather than reading "I'm feeling pretty hungry all of a sudden. How about getting something to eat?" you will actually be able to see through the words and see the underlying statement "feed me now."

Speed perceiving

When you break down the nuts and bolts of speed reading, you discover that a better term might, in fact, be speed *perceiving*. The main reason for this is that while certain techniques within speed reading will teach you to read words at a faster rate, most will, in fact, teach you to read fewer words altogether. Since most words are only filler, it makes sense to ignore them and focus solely on those words that contain valuable information. This is the essence of speed reading. As you develop the various speed reading skills, you won't be solely fixated on your reading speed. Instead, you will see reading in a whole new light. Sure, there will be times when you will want to read a document word for word, specifically when you are reading for pleasure. After all, poetry simply isn't the same if you skim through it for the pertinent information. And since most works of fiction spend copious amounts of words describing a situation your reading experience will be richer if you take the time and effort to read all of the words.

However, most of the material you read probably won't be for pleasure. Instead, much of it will be for learning specific information and acquiring particular insights. Newspapers are a prime example of this. You really don't need to know all of the sensational details about a particular thing that happened. Simply knowing when, where and how it happened is often enough. Speed reading is the ability to look at a newspaper and take away only the vital information without being dragged down by the countless words used to sensationalize the story. Furthermore, when you master the speed reading skill set you will be able to read business spreadsheets, memorandums, technical data and any other sort of informative document with greater speed, clarity and increased retention. This will make you highly valuable in any business environment. Rather than filling your mind with unnecessary filler and fluff you will be able to pinpoint the pertinent information and move on while others are still meandering through the endless stream of words. This is the true nature and purpose of speed reading.

Chapter 2: Assessing Your Reading Habits

Before you begin learning the different techniques of speed reading, it is necessary to assess your current reading habits. One of the main reasons for this is that different speed reading techniques are designed to break particular bad habits with regard to reading and replace them with better habits. Therefore, it is important to discover which bad habits you practice regularly in order to ensure that you choose the speed reading techniques that will benefit you the most.

Another reason why it is important to assess your reading habits is so that you can create realistic goals for yourself. If you approach speed reading without a clear idea of what you want to achieve your results will be less measurable and meaningful. Only when you determine how you want to change your reading style can you begin to take the necessary steps toward achieving that goal. Therefore, the first thing you need to do is to closely observe how you read. This includes your reading speed, your eye movements, how easily distracted you are and whether or not you vocalize words as you read them. By recognizing how each of these aspects affects your reading abilities, you will be able to tailor make a specific speed reading regimen that will break your bad habits and provide you with the results you desire.

Determine your reading speed

As mentioned earlier, the average person's reading speed is about 200 words per minute. However, this isn't to say that this is your reading speed. The fact is that each person has a unique reading style, and this style has a direct impact on how many words you are able to read on average. The first thing you need to do, therefore, is to determine your reading speed so that you know where you are in comparison to where you want to be.

There are a few different methods for measuring your reading speed. All of these methods require the use of a timer, however, so it is important that you have a timer available. You can use a stopwatch, a kitchen timer or any other kind of timer that has a bell or an alarm to tell you when to stop. If you don't possess any of these timers you should check your cell phone as just about every cell phone has a timer app. Worst case scenario you can buy a timer for only a few dollars at any grocery store.

Once you have a timer, the next thing to get is something to read. You can use anything at all, including a magazine, newspaper, book or even something online. The important thing is that you are comfortable with whatever it is you are going to read. Once you have your reading material you need to do a word count. You can take the time to count the exact number of words on a page, however, a rough estimate is enough for this exercise. To estimate how many words are on a page simply count the number of words in a single line. Then count the number of lines per page and multiply the two numbers. Thus, if there are 18 words per line and 30 lines per page your estimation would be 30 x 18, which equals 540. The next thing to do is set your timer to either count up or for more time than you will need to read the page. Since the average rate is 200 words per minute you can set your timer for 4 minutes, more than enough time for 540 words. Start your timer and read the page. When you have finished reading stop the timer and see how long you took.

Another way to determine your reading speed is to set a timer for 2 minutes and read as much as you can before the timer goes off. When your time expires you can count the number of words you read and divide by 2 for the number of words you read per minute. This is an easier way to get a precise count of words per minute as you use a precise measure of time rather than a precise number of words. In any event, both methods will allow you to get a sense of your average reading speed, and this is a critical thing to know in order to get the best results when trying to increase your reading speed.

Observe your eye movements

The next thing you need to observe is your eye movements while you read. Most people have the mistaken idea that they simply move their eyes along a line of text at a smooth and steady pace, rarely fluctuating. The truth is that your eye movements are probably quite jerky and irregular, going forward from one group of words to another, and even back again to reread something for clarity or context. Focusing your eyes on a word or group of words is referred to as "fixation." Moving your eyes from one word to another, or from one group of words to another, is called a "saccade." When it comes to speed reading, it is just as important to know how your eyes move as it is to know your reading speed.

Determining your eye movements is a pretty easy process. Simply read one line of text and count the number of times you move your eyes. Be sure to include all movement, including forward, backward and even any time you glance over to something else altogether. Each and every time you move your eyes is important, so be sure to count everything. You can read more than one line of text if you want, however reading one is enough to get an idea of how much time and energy you waste moving your eyes unnecessarily.

The next step is to classify your eye movements. If your count revealed that you moved your eyes eight times while reading a line of text you need to break that number down into the different types of eye movement. How many of those eight times were moving forward, how many were moving back and how many were distracted glances to something else? This shows how much energy you spend fixating on words, a habit that speed reading will break you off. If the number of times you move your eyes is relatively low you won't have too much work to do. Additionally, if you rarely or never went backwards to reread text then you are doing pretty well already. However, you will probably discover that, like most people, your eyes move all over the place when you read. Needless to say, this significantly reduces your reading speed as well as your reading comprehension.

Do you vocalize words as you read them?

The chances are that as you are reading these words you are vocalizing them in your mind. This is a classic reading habit that is responsible for the average person having such a slow reading speed. Unfortunately, it is also one of the hardest habits to break. This is due to how the habit was formed in the first place. More often than not, the reason why a person vocalizes the words they read is that they were trained to do so. If you think back to when you learned how to read you will probably recall that your teacher had you read out loud at first. This was done so that your teacher could make sure you were pronouncing words correctly. After a while, when you proved that you could pronounce each and every word properly your teacher would tell you to stop reading out loud. They probably said something along the lines of "say it with your mind, not your mouth." And thus, the habit of vocalizing as you read was born.

Unfortunately, the age at which this instruction came along was one in which the average person is most impressionable. That is why this habit is so hard to break. Still, the important thing at this stage is to determine whether or not you commit this "reading crime." The main reason why this is such a problem is that it takes your mind longer to vocalize a word than it does to simply see a word. Therefore, as long as you "speak" the words in your mind you will never be able to improve your reading speed beyond a certain point, normally around 300 words per minute. Fortunately, there are several speed reading techniques that will help you to break this harmful habit.

Are you focused?

Finally, there is the question of how focused you are when you read. In order to determine this element choose something to read, set a timer for 5 minutes and read until the timer goes off. During this time count how many times you shift your attention from what you are reading to something else. Even if it is something else on the page, such as another line of text, a picture or a smudge mark, it counts. Needless to say, if you look up from your text that definitely counts! Simply count the number of times you are distracted in the 5 minute period. If this number is low then you already have good focus, therefore this isn't something you need to work on initially. However, if the number is high, such as 20 or more, then focus is something you will need to work on right away. The reason this is so important is that it takes your mind time to refocus on what you are reading each time you are distracted, which significantly lowers your reading speed. Fortunately, there are many speed reading tricks and techniques to help you fix this problem.

Chapter 3: Breaking Bad Reading Habits

As with anything in life, the first thing you need to do in order to move forward with speed reading is eliminate the things that are holding you back. Bad habits are just as common in reading as they are in anything else. And, just as bad habits can keep a person from losing weight, getting a better job, or making any other significant improvement in their life, so too, they will keep you from successfully developing your speed reading skills. Therefore, before you start learning the different techniques that will greatly increase your reading speed and comprehension you must first identify and remove any bad reading habits you currently have. Don't be too disheartened if you suffer from most or all of the habits listed in this chapter. The truth is that these habits are very common to the vast majority of people, so you aren't alone! Fortunately, there are several simple yet effective methods for breaking these bad reading habits. This chapter will reveal those methods, thus enabling you to begin eliminating your bad reading habits right away.

Eliminate distractions

One of the main reasons why most people read at a slower speed is that they never pay full attention to what they are reading. The fact is that the brain can actually change its focus while you are reading, thereby causing the other senses to become heightened. As a result, your hearing, sense of smell and even sense of taste can begin to become more noticeable than normal, creating all sorts of distractions for your mind. The main reason for this is that when you read your eyes become focused on one thing instead of the countless things they normally see. This reduction in visual input causes your mind to look for input elsewhere. It's the same dynamic that occurs when you close your eyes. Therefore, it is critical that you take the necessary steps to eliminate any distractions that your other senses might pick up on.

Always make sure that you are reading in a relatively quiet place in order to avoid being distracted by different noises. One of the biggest mistakes most people make when reading is to read with a TV or radio on in the background. It is virtually impossible to focus on what you are reading when you have constant dialogue taking place for your ears to pick up on. Music can be a help or a hindrance depending on the person, so take the time to see if background music helps you to focus or if it distracts your attention. Other senses, such as your sense of taste and smell can be easily distracted if you are hungry. Therefore, always make sure you address such issues as being hungry or thirsty before settling down to read.

Another source of distraction can come from your mind itself. If you have an appointment later in the day you will become increasingly conscientious of the time, thereby creating a mental distraction that keeps you from fully focusing on what you are reading. Likewise, any to-do lists will tend to roll through your mind, constantly reminding you not to forget such things as going to the grocery store, answering an email, or any number of similar tasks. The best way to avoid such distractions is to take care of these tasks before you try to read any lengthy material. Only when your mind is clear of distractions will you be able to read at optimum efficiency.

How to stop word vocalization

As mentioned earlier, the act of vocalizing words as you read will significantly reduce your reading speed. This is because the average person can only speak at around 300 words per minute.

Therefore, by vocalizing your words you create a fixed barrier that your reading speed will never be able to exceed. The good news is that even though this habit is both highly common and highly disruptive it can be broken. It will, however, take both time and effort to break completely. But it can be done.

The first method to breaking word vocalization is to create a distraction. This may seem counter intuitive since distractions can hinder your reading speed, however, a small distraction can stop the vocalization without having any negative side effects. One such distraction is to chew a piece of gum. The act of chewing will keep your mind from vocalizing words by tricking it. Simply put, when your mouth is chewing your mind will be less likely to vocalize anything since you might not be able to actually speak. In a way it's a bit like your mind practicing good manners. Since it's rude to talk while eating, your mind stops vocalizing while you are chewing. A piece of gum can keep you chewing for quite some time, thus enabling you to get a good bit of speed reading done without the inner dialogue.

Another distraction that can eliminate vocalizing the words you read is to listen to music while you read. Again, this will work better for some people as others might become too distracted by music. The important thing is to test different types of music in order to find one that does the trick. Something that most people find is that strictly instrumental music proves less distracting than music with vocals. This is because your mind tends to focus on any speech that it hears. Therefore, as instrumental music is free of speech it will be less distracting in a negative way. It will, however, create enough of a distraction to keep you from vocalizing written material.

If none of these methods helps to eliminate the inner dialogue you can always try counting while you read. This is the most complicated method, but it is one that tends to work when all else fails. The reason behind this is that you are breaking your habit of vocalizing the words you read by vocalizing something else, in this case counting. Once you develop the ability to read while counting in your mind you have effectively broken your habit of vocalizing what you read. The next step is to stop counting while you read, and then you're cured!

Learning to minimize eye movement while reading

Studies have shown that as the average person reads their eyes move in jerky motions in just about every direction. When moving forward your eyes will jump from the word you are reading to another word further down the line. This random and erratic motion serves to significantly reduce anyone's reading speed. The simple truth of the matter is that you only read when your eyes are still. Therefore, the more your eyes move is the less you actually read. Thus, learning to minimize your eye movements is absolutely critical if you want to become a proficient speed reader.

The first method for learning to reduce your eye movement is to train your eyes to only move to certain points along any line of text. While you might think that you can only see one word at a time the fact is that your periphery vision allows you to see up to five or six words at once. Data collected from numerous studies suggests that you can see a couple of words to your left, and three to four to your right. This means that you can read an entire line of text by only focusing on a set number of spots along the line. If the line has twenty words you can read it with as few as three eye movements. Learning this process will increase your reading speed exponentially.

Perhaps the easiest and most effective method of training your eyes this way is to use an index card. Place the card over the line you are going to read and mark an 'x' over the first word. Place another 'x' four words further along. Repeat this for the length of the line. Once you have your card marked read the line by focusing your eyes only on the words below each 'x.' At first, this will be a bit strange, so you might not read all the words on the line. However, with a little practice you will develop your peripheral awareness, thus allowing you to see and take in the words your eyes aren't focused on. Eventually, you will be able to extend your markings, putting an 'x' over every fifth or sixth word. This process is known as "chunking," and it breaks you from the habit of focusing on each and every word of text. When you read "chunks" of words at a time it also helps to break you of vocalizing what you read, so it provides two benefits in one.

Breaking the habit of regression reading

The final habit that keeps most people from developing a good reading speed is that of regression reading. This is the act of skipping back to re-read text in order to better understand it. Needless to say, if you take one step back for every two steps forward it will take you that much longer to make any real progress. Unfortunately, most people have this habit, and it keeps them from achieving their true reading potential.

The good news is that this is probably the easiest habit to break. One simple method is to cover over the words you read as you read them. When the words are no longer visible you are less tempted to go back and look at them again. This process might slow your reading down a bit as you have to conscientiously keep up with covering the words you read, but it is an exercise that will be short lived. Once you break yourself of the temptation of re-reading text you can stop covering the words as you go. You don't have to cover more than the last few words to have the effect, so an index card will do just fine for the task.

Another way to avoid re-reading text is to use a pointer to "pull" you along the line of text. This is a method usually associated with increasing reading speed, but it can also serve to help keep you focused on the material ahead rather than the material behind. Again, you don't have to read with your finger moving along the lines of text forever, you only need to use this method until you break the habit of re-reading previous text. In the end you will discover that as you read forward any ambiguities or questions will be answered eventually, making regression reading completely unnecessary. More often than not pertinent information is repeated in any given text, therefore if you didn't get the information on the first time of reading you will get it again later on. Furthermore, context clues can help clarify questions throughout a written text, making it unnecessary to absorb each and every word along the way.

Chapter 4: Creating Good Reading Habits

Now that you know the most common bad reading habits and how to overcome them it's time to start developing good reading habits. When you free yourself of the things holding you back and begin to practice positive habits and techniques you will unleash your true reading potential. Not only will you be able to read at a faster pace, but by practicing good reading habits you will increase your ability to disseminate and retain valuable information contained in any written text. Some of the most effective and commonly used good reading techniques may prove easier and less complex than you might expect. In fact, most good reading habits come down to nothing more than basic common sense. This chapter will reveal four of the best reading habits you can form to improve both your reading speed and comprehension.

Choose the right place and time

One of the biggest mistakes that most people make when it comes to reading is the time of day they choose to read in. Everyone knows that a person's physical energy levels fluctuate during the day, making certain times better for physical exertion than others. You wouldn't expect to find that mowing a lawn at midnight would prove as easy as if you performed the task during the early afternoon. Darkness aside, the fact is that you don't have the same energy at midnight as you do during the earlier hours of the day. Therefore, any task that requires physical exertion will prove more difficult as your energy levels decrease. The very same principle applies to mental exertion. Just as your physical energy is higher during the early hours of the morning, so is your mental energy higher as well. Thus, any mental activity will prove more difficult to perform late at night than it would have been during the earlier part of the day.

Subsequently, if you want to read with increased effectiveness and efficiency you need to choose a time when your mental energy is at its peak. While it's true that no two people are exactly alike, and thus, your energy levels may peak at different times, it's highly likely that your mind will be most attentive and capable during the late morning and early afternoon hours of the day. Even so, it's always best to discover your personal design in order to get the best results from your efforts. You can try reading at different times of the day to see which times work best for you. Things you want to look for include how focused you are, how easily you can read the material, how quickly you can read the material and how much information you are able to retain. Once you find your best reading time it is important that you set that time aside for any lengthy or serious reading that you need to do.

Of equal importance to when you read is where you read. All too often people expect to be able to read anywhere just as they expect to be able to read at any time. Unfortunately, when you read in the wrong environment your attention can be seriously distracted, making reading an almost impossible task. Therefore, it is vital that you discover what environments work best for you when you need to do some serious reading. You might expect that the best place to read is somewhere quiet and isolated, however, this isn't necessarily true. While some people will find such environments ideal for reading others will find too much isolation or too much silence unsettling, creating considerable distraction as a result. Again, it is important that you take the time to discover what works for you. Read in several different places with different amounts of activity and noise. Once you discover the right environment for you make sure you do your reading in that environment whenever possible.

Choose the right material

Even though people's mental energy is higher earlier in the day than it is late at night, that isn't to suggest that you shouldn't read anything at night. Instead, it means that certain types of material should be avoided. Many people like to read before going to bed as it helps them to unwind and relax. However, if you choose this time to read an academic text or some sort of instructional material you will find your efforts all but wasted. The key is to choose the right material for different times of day. Any text that requires serious concentration and thought should be reserved for the times of day when your mind is at its strongest. Not only will this ensure that you read the material more quickly and easily, it also means that you will understand any valuable information it contains more readily.

Any night time reading should be restricted to fiction or light reading that requires less concentration than more academic texts. This type of writing is designed to activate the imagination more than the intellect, and thus it will be easier to read at the end of the day when your intellectual mind is tired and ready to rest. In fact, some people find it a struggle to read fiction during the day as their mind is more ready for an intellectual challenge than for engaging in fantasy and imagination. Still, these are generalizations, and the bottom line is that you need to find what works best for you. Try reading different types of texts at different times of day to determine which times prove best for each one. Then try to ensure that you read the right materials at the right times.

Learn to read content instead of words

If you read a book for the sake of relaxing and letting your mind drift off into the realm of fantasy then reading a text word for word is not necessarily a bad thing. However, if you are reading a text in order to acquire specific information then reading it word for word can, in fact, be a profound waste of time and energy. The simple truth is that there are two types of reading. First, there is reading for the sake of reading. This usually covers such genres as fiction, poetry and the like where each word can be instrumental at setting a scene or creating a mood. The second type of reading is reading for information. This is the type of reading you engage in when doing research, catching up on the news or reading instructional texts. It is also the type where reading word for word is totally unnecessary.

The trick to speed reading content for information is that you look for keywords. This allows you to see the content without having to pick through each and every word in the process. One way to ensure that you focus on content rather than words is to have a list of words that you are looking for. More often than not you will be looking to discover specific information within a given text. If you read the entire text you will wind up reading all sorts of information you didn't actually want or need. However, if you look for the information you need you can glance at a text and find it immediately. By focusing solely on the portions of text that contain the information you need you can reduce the amount of reading you do by up to seventy five percent. This is the act of reading content rather than words.

Exercise your mind

Finally, there is the factor that separates the true speed readers from all the rest. This is the habit of exercising your mind. Just as a person's body becomes stronger and capable of doing more as a result of physical exercise, so too, a person's mind reacts the same way to mental exercise. The more you exercise your mind is, the stronger and more capable it will become. Fortunately, it takes less time and effort to exercise the mind than it does to exercise the body. In fact, if you follow two specific exercises you will achieve any speed reading results you hope for with considerable speed and ease.

The first exercise is to increase your vocabulary. While a person's reading speed is usually reduced by such things as distraction, bad reading habits and the like the truth is that it can also be reduced by a small vocabulary. If you don't know a word, you will likely trip over it when you read it, as though it were a piece of furniture out of place. Therefore it is critical that you take the time and effort to increase your vocabulary knowledge in order to increase your reading efficiency. Fortunately, there are several ways in which you can achieve this goal. Daily calendars are available that have a different word each and every day, helping you to build your vocabulary in a relaxed but constant way. There are also online sources that offer a word a day or other such formats that introduce new words at a steady yet reasonable pace.

The second best exercise for your mind is simply reading more. As with every other thing in life, when it comes to reading practice makes perfect. People with the lowest reading speeds are often people who read the least amount of material. Alternatively, the more a person reads is, the better their reading speed and comprehension becomes. Therefore, perhaps the most critical element for developing the skill set of speed reading is your familiarity with reading itself. The more you read it, the more your mind will be comfortable with the process. Reading more will also help you to practice speed reading techniques more frequently, enabling you to master them even faster as a result.

Chapter 5: Proven Speed Reading Techniques

The next step toward developing your speed reading skills is to begin practicing the most effective speed reading techniques. While there are several different techniques that can help to increase your reading speed and comprehension it only takes a few to make all the difference. In fact, it is recommended that instead of trying to learn all the techniques at once you should start with one or two, choosing to master those techniques before moving on to practicing the others. The following four methods are among the most proven speed reading techniques practiced by the pros. Once you begin practicing these methods you will notice results that are both immediate and highly significant. Needless to say, the more you practice these methods is, the better the results you will achieve. Some studies have shown that your reading speed will increase exponentially in as few as five weeks when you practice these methods each and every day.

Skim passages for pertinent information

One of the most widely used techniques within speed reading is what is called skimming. While the idea of skimming text may seem straightforward the fact is that it is often confused with its popular counterpart scanning. When you skim a text you read over the content looking for the important information contained within. Most of the time you won't necessarily know what this information is, meaning that you can't simply look for specific keywords. Instead you have to discover the information as you read along. This means that you will have to read a good percentage of the text, however, it does not mean that you have to read all of the text.

A simple method of scanning text is to read the first and last paragraphs of a section of text. This is easier to do when reading non-fiction as you can't necessarily skip entire stretches of fiction without losing important context and plot details. However, in the case of non-fiction material where information is usually addressed at the beginning of a section and reviewed at the end you can get all the details you need by reading these portions and skipping the middle altogether. The only thing you will miss by skipping middle portions is the exhaustive explanations of the topic being discussed. All pertinent information will be spelled out at the end, making that the most important piece of any non-fiction text.

The best way to skim a text is to come up with a list of questions in your mind regarding the information you are looking for. Such questions as *who, why, when* and *how* are the most useful when trying to get to the heart of a particular topic. If you can answer all of your questions after reading the beginning and end of a section then you know that you have obtained all the information you need, thus allowing you to move on. In addition to reading the beginning and end paragraphs you can also skim the headings of a section, descriptions below pictures, the table of contents and any other piece of text, which might contain condensed information. Sometimes you can get the gist of an article simply by reading its headings, subheadings and any bullet points contained within. This can save you from reading countless amounts of unnecessary text that only serves to increase the bulk of an article.

Scan text for keywords

Scanning is another proven technique for speed reading. While scanning may appear almost identical to skimming at first there is a very basic yet significant difference. When you skim a text you are looking for information that is unfamiliar to you. However, when you scan a text you are looking for information that you already know. One of the best examples of this is when you look for a particular movie or TV show in a list such as on Netflix or in the TV listings. When you are looking for something specific you pass over all of the information that doesn't match what you are looking for, making your search quick and efficient. Imagine how long it would take to find a movie or TV show if you actually took the time to read each and every word you came across. By the time you found what you were looking for it would have ended hours ago! Instead, you skip over non-essential text, searching instead for specific keywords, pictures or names. This is the art of scanning.

This practice is ordinarily used for locating specific information within a text for immediate use. Names, addresses, times and other detailed information are some of the more common examples of this type of information. Therefore, scanning isn't necessarily a technique you will use in regular reading, rather it is a technique that will only be used in specific circumstances. You can also scan a text to determine whether or not it contains enough pertinent information to actually read in greater depth. This is a highly effective technique for anyone doing research on a particular topic. Rather than reading countless articles you can narrow down your search by scanning each resource to determine its overall value. Not only will this save you time but it will also ensure that the reading you do is more productive.

Again, like with skimming you can focus on the beginning and end of a text, headings, tables, picture captions and the like. Since you are looking for specific keywords you will be able to scan any size text with a great deal of speed and ease. The more keywords that you find is, the more valuable a particular text will be. Alternatively, if you are unable to locate many or any keywords after a fair amount of scanning it is probably a safe bet that you should move on to another resource.

Change the order in which you read

Sometimes you might find that you have to read an entire text for one reason or another, meaning that scanning or skimming is out of the question. In such cases it might be tempting to simply revert to your old habit of reading a text word for word in the order it's written. Fortunately, there is a technique that can allow you to read a text completely yet with greater speed and understanding. This technique is changing the order in which you read. As mentioned earlier, most of the pertinent information in an article or informative text is contained in the beginning and end of the piece. Thus, if you read the beginning and end you will become familiar with the topic even if you previously had no knowledge of the topic at all. Once you have familiarized yourself with the material in this way you can read the middle portion with greater speed and ease. Since you will recognize the terms and concepts you can digest the more exhaustive text without any problems whatsoever. Therefore, if you have to read an entire text that is filled with detailed information, always read the beginning and end before reading the middle.

Another strategy is to read all of the information about the text that is available. Most books will have a brief description covering the content of the book, the author and any pertinent details about the topic being discussed. Most people skip such descriptions, viewing them as nothing more than promotional pieces designed to encourage a person to buy the book. However, skilled speed readers will recognize the value of these parts for the condensed information that they contain. In a way, reading any descriptive piece on a text is like watching the trailer of a movie. While the trailer doesn't provide the full content of the movie it gives you an idea of the characters, the plot and more often than not the outcome. When you go to see the movie after seeing its trailer you already have a sense of what to expect, allowing you to enjoy the subtle nuances of the movie that much more. This is the very same benefit you will gain when you read a description of a text before reading the text itself.

Read with purpose

In the end it comes down to one simple concept—reading with purpose. Whether you scan a text, skim a text or change the order in which you read a complete text, the key is to read for a specific reason. What slows most people down in their reading is that they read for the sake of reading, not for the sake of gathering information. However, when you read for the sole purpose of gathering information you will find that your reading habits change completely, allowing you to read in a fraction of the time while obtaining more information in the process.

Shopping is a great analogy for this. There are two basic types of shopping—window-shopping and hunting. When a person window-shops they tend to look at everything with little or no intention of actually buying what they see. They can spend all day window-shopping and not feel as though they have wasted any time. This is because they had no real agenda to start with. Instead, they simply wanted to spend their time wandering from one store to the next, seeing everything that is available. This is how most people read. They look at all of the words, taking everything in at an equal rate. Rather than looking for specific information they look at all the information, willing to take all the time in the world in the process.

Alternatively, there is the type of shopping known as hunting. This is when a person is on a mission to find and acquire a specific item. They may go to several stores in an attempt to find the best form of the item at the best price, but this is different from window-shopping. Even if the person goes to more than one store they won't spend much time in each, rather they will look to see if their item is available and if it's available for the right price. If it's not there, or if it's too expensive, they leave the store and move on to the next. Reading with purpose is like hunting. Instead of spending large amounts of time meandering through endless amounts of text you search for specific information. If a text contains that information you read it, but only as much as is necessary. If a text doesn't contain the information you leave it and move on. Just as a hunting-style shopping trip can take minutes as opposed to the hours spent window-shopping, so too, reading with purpose will reduce the time it takes to a readable text to a fraction of what it would take otherwise. Furthermore, you will always leave with exactly what you need—nothing more and nothing less.

Chapter 6: Creating Your Daily Reading Practice

The importance of continuously practicing speed reading techniques cannot be overstated. Developing any skill requires constant work and dedication, and speed reading is certainly no exception to that rule. A good way to envision your speed reading development is to liken it to becoming a bodybuilder. One of the most effective ways of developing stronger muscles is to exercise on a regular basis. Equally important is to use the right exercises for your particular goals. Since some techniques for speed reading are designed for certain texts it is vital that you determine the type of reading you do in order to identify which speed reading techniques will be most beneficial for you. This chapter breaks down the different types of reading so that you can develop a daily routine that will help you to gain the best speed reading results possible. Whether you choose one or more of the techniques listed below, the most important thing is that you commit to practicing them on a daily basis. That is the only way to achieve the results you desire and deserve.

How to practice speed reading books

If you are the type of person who reads more fiction than anything else you will need to use the speed reading techniques that focus on reading an entire text more quickly and efficiently. One technique already mentioned is that of chunking words. This method requires a great deal of practice as it not only causes you to read faster, but it also causes you to read in a completely different way. The best way to practice this method is as follows:

- **Choose a simple text**. Just as a person who is new to lifting weights will start with lighter weights, so too, when you start practicing speed reading techniques you should begin with easier texts. The font size should be large enough to be able to read easily, and the words should be simple enough for you to understand. If you begin with a complicated text you will struggle with the text as well as the exercise, making your progress slower and more complicated than it has to be.

- **Start slow**. Chunking words is a method that you build over time. Rather than trying to read five or six words at once start by trying to just read two words at a time. This will help you to become familiar with the process without being overwhelmed by it. As you become accustomed to reading two words at a time you can increase it to three, then eventually four and even five.

- **Set a goal**. Another way to control the progress you make is to set solid goals for yourself. In the case of chunking words, you can set yourself the goal of becoming proficient at reading two words at a time in seven days. Take the next seven days to achieve the ability to read three words at a time. If you give yourself a week to develop each level you can progress at a steady yet significant pace. While a month may seem like a long time to complete this goal you have to realize that at the end of that month you will be reading four to five times faster than you do now. That's a pretty decent result to say the least!

- **Set aside quality time**. If you try to practice at different times of day, and in different environments, you will find your progress slower and less consistent. Therefore, it is critical that you set aside some quality time each and every day for your practice. By practicing at the same time and in the same conditions you can focus all of your energy on the exercise, thereby ensuring that you achieve the best results for your efforts.

How to practice speed reading news articles

Reading news articles is a different thing altogether from reading fictional texts. This means that the techniques needed for speed reading news articles will also be different. Skimming is probably the best method for getting pertinent information from any news oriented text, regardless of whether it's a newspaper, online article or some other similar format. The best way to practice skimming is as follows:

- **Create a list of questions**. As mentioned earlier, the best way to get information while skimming a text is to look for answers to specific questions. Therefore, the first thing you want to practice is the art of creating the questions. The best way to do this is to look at a news headline and ask what information you want to know about that particular topic. Once you have that list, read the entire article, without any concern over speed. Write down the pertinent information and compare it to your list. Did your questions cover everything or did you miss something? At first you might miss a question or two, however, when you practice this exercise a few times you will get the hang of knowing exactly what questions to ask in order to get all the important information.

- **Practice skimming.** Once you know what questions to ask you can begin to practice skimming in its entirety. Pick a news article, list your questions and skim for the answers. Focus on highlighted areas such as headlines, picture captions, quotes and any other text that stands out from the rest. See if you can't find all your answers in these key areas.

- **Build your speed**. Sometimes you will have to read entire portions of text in order to acquire the information you need. In this case you will want to practice reading lines of text quickly, usually using your finger as a guide to lead over the words in a quick and uniform way. The important element is gaining information, so only read as fast as you can while still being able to recognize important pieces of information as you come to them. As you develop this skill your speed will automatically increase, so you don't have to focus on it as much. Just remember, daily practice is the key to building your speed, so as long as you put in the effort you will get the results.

How to practice speed reading informational texts

Reading informational texts is similar to reading news articles, however, you will probably have some familiarity with the nature of the information you are looking for in this case. Subsequently, scanning is the method you will want to practice for this type of reading. As previously discussed, the key difference between skimming and scanning is that you will have a list of keywords to look for with scanning that you didn't have in the case of skimming. This makes all the difference between the two methods. The best way to practice scanning is as follows:

- **Identify primary targets**. The first thing you want to learn is what parts of a text are more likely to contain the information you are looking for. Take an article that you are already familiar with and come up with a list of keywords you know the article contains. Next, read the whole article, noting where each keyword is found. You can use a highlighter or simply circle the words as you find them. When you have read the whole article look at where the highlighted or circled words are. You will notice that they are clustered rather than spread out. Do this again on two or three other articles. In the end, you will notice a pattern as to where the keywords are most commonly located. These areas will be your primary targets.

- **Practice scanning unfamiliar articles**. Now that you have your primary targets identified you can see how effective they truly are by reading articles you are unfamiliar with. It is important that you have certain keywords to look for in these articles, however, as that is what is needed to perform the technique of scanning. When you have your keywords listed find as many as you can using only the primary targets. If you didn't find all of the words decide whether the missing ones are actually necessary, or whether the ones you found were enough. If the missing ones are necessary read the whole article in order to locate them. This will give you an idea of other targets to look for when scanning unfamiliar texts.

- **Build your speed**. Finally, practice scanning in a timed run. You can set a timer for one minute to start with, seeing if you can find all your keywords within that time. Once you can achieve that goal on a regular basis you can reduce the time by five seconds at a time. Eventually, you will be able to scan an article for as little as twenty seconds, obtaining all of the pertinent information you need within that time.

The need for discipline

It goes without saying that discipline is the key to achieving any level of success in any endeavor. Only when you put in constant effort and dedication can you hope to reach any goal. However, there can be many sides to discipline that are often overlooked. The key areas of discipline needed for developing your speed reading skills are as follows:

- **Practice daily**. You will have read these words several times already within this book, and you will probably read them several times more before the end. The main reason for that is because this is the most important element of developing your speed reading skills. If you stop practicing for any significant length of time you will begin to regress, meaning that your progress is not only slowed but actually reversed. Therefore, make sure that you practice each and every day so that your skills only ever get stronger.

- **Practice at a reasonable rate.** Sometimes you might be tempted to rush in and try to achieve results in less time by skipping steps or increasing the level of the challenge. While this won't be as dangerous as if you skipped ahead and began lifting heavier weights than you were ready for in the case of bodybuilding, it will still prove foolish. Developing any skill is a matter of progression. You need to learn to walk before you can run. Therefore, give yourself the right amount of time to ensure that you develop your skills properly.

- **Repeat steps when necessary.** Certain skills will require more time than others. This is simply due to the fact that different people have different inherent abilities that enable them to excel at certain things. However, there will be some things you don't excel at. If you need to repeat a step or add time on to a particular practice, then do so. Never push on for the sake of pushing on. Always make sure that you have fully developed each skill before starting on the next. It takes considerable discipline to know when you aren't ready to move on.

Chapter 7: Some Simple Exercises

There may be times when you aren't able to read much on a particular day. It stands to reason that your schedule might change unexpectedly from time to time, disrupting your day-to-day routine. Fortunately, this isn't necessarily a problem. In the event that you can't devote the time and energy to reading your regular amount of material you can choose to perform quick and easy exercises to help keep your speed reading skills sharp. The following are some examples of these exercises, along with some additional online tools that will help improve your speed reading development.

Practice reading with a timer

This is an easy exercise that can be performed with any of the speed reading techniques covered. You can choose to read a portion of text within a given amount of time to ensure your reading rate is at its peak, or you can test yourself on such techniques as skimming or scanning to determine your rate at acquiring specific information. The important thing is to develop a timed exercise that suits your needs. In the event that you read regular text you can set a timer for two minutes and count the number of words you have read within that time. Even though this may not seem like much it will help to keep your mind ready and focused for when you do return to reading lengthier passages.

When it comes to practicing timed runs with skimming and scanning the focus is on information rather than word count. Set a timer for sixty seconds and skim or scan your chosen document. When the timer goes off see if you have acquired all of the necessary information.

Needless to say, the time you set will decrease as your skills improve, thus the sixty second time is just an example. You may want to set the time for thirty seconds to give you an extra challenge. If you have a timer app on your phone or a timer on your watch you can perform this exercise anytime, anywhere. You can even practice while in a waiting room, online at the supermarket, or even waiting for a train. All you need is access to an informative document, a timer and a moment to yourself.

Highly effective eye exercises

One thing that can help to increase your speed reading results is to regularly exercise your eyes. This makes perfect sense since it's your eyes that are doing all of the physical work. If your eyes are weak your reading speed will suffer as a result. Therefore, increasing the health and strength of your eyes is a vital process with regard to improving your speed reading skills. The following are a few examples of eye exercises that you can do anytime and anywhere:

- **Eye squeezes**. This exercise should actually be called "face squeezes" as it addresses the muscles in your face and neck as well. You can do this exercise any time you have three or so minutes of uninterrupted time to spare. First, slowly take in a deep breath, opening your mouth and eyes as wide as possible in order to stretch your facial muscles. Next, exhale slowly, closing your eyes as tightly as you can while also squeezing the muscles of your head, neck, face and jaw. Maintain this position while holding your breath for about 30 seconds. Repeat the process three or four more times for best results.

- **Eye writing**. This exercise strengthens your eyes by making them move in ways they are unaccustomed to. Most of the time your eyes move up and down or side to side. However, this exercise will increase the range of your eye motion by making your eyes move in various directions. First, focus on a wall that is fairly far away from you. Next, pretend that you are using your eyes to write your name on the wall. In other words, move your eyes along the same way you would a pen when writing your name. The different motions will increase the strength and dexterity of your eyes.

- **Thumb-to-thumb glancing**. This exercise is similar to eye writing, although it focuses solely on the side-to-side motion of your eyes. Start by looking straight ahead, extending your arms to your sides. Stick your thumbs straight up, as though you are hitching a ride. Next, look back and forth between your left thumb and your right thumb ten times without moving your head. Rest your eyes for 30 seconds and repeat three more times.

Test your comprehension

As mentioned earlier, speed reading is as much about comprehension as it is about speed. Being able to read 600 words per minute is of no value if you don't understand or retain what you read. Therefore, you will want to test your comprehension as often as you test your reading speed. This is a fairly simple process, requiring nothing more than answering a few questions after you read a portion of text. In fact, you can incorporate this test with the timed reading tests. After you complete a timed run on reading, skimming or scanning take a moment to ask yourself the nature of what you just read. If you are reading a work of fiction try to recall the events you read in as much detail as possible. List off the characters involved, the locations, and any events that took place. The more detailed your recollection is, the better since this shows that you have a high comprehension rate.

When you test your skimming and scanning using a timed run you will automatically test your comprehension when you try to list the information you obtained at the end of the exercise. In the case of skimming you should be able to answer the basic questions of who, why, where, what and how. If you cannot answer any of these questions you can either increase the time you set for your runs, or you can keep practicing with the shorter time. When you can answer all of the questions within the time allotted you can reduce the time, thereby developing your skills even further.

Additional tools for improving your skills

There are an increasing number of online apps that will help you to hone your speed reading skills. Each app offers a different range of tools and text availability, so it is important that you take the time to research each app in order to know the one that is best suited to your needs. Furthermore, not all apps are compatible with all devices, so be sure to check compatibility before making your purchase. Here are four of the more popular speed reading apps available:

- **ReadMe**. ReadMe is an e-reader app that can be integrated with other speed reading tools to help you to increase your reading speed quickly and easily. You can store your personal library onto ReadMe, which will enable you to speed read familiar material. When used with BeeLine Reader your material will have color added to the words, effectively guiding your eyes along the lines of text in a natural and effective way. This will increase your reading speed while training your eyes to avoid regression reading. When used with Spritz you can read your favorite books one word at a time, with each word being flashed onto the screen so that you can reduce your eye movement to an absolute minimum. It is compatible with both iPhone and Android devices.

- **Accelerator**. Unlike ReadMe, Accelerator does not act as a personal library. The main function of this app is to enable you to speed read news articles, text documents from your personal email account or certain online news and article apps. This app is reminiscent of the reading tests many people get in grade school where a document scrolls along at a set pace, determining your reading speed. The pace is adjustable, so you can use this app to increase and monitor your reading rate. This app is only compatible with iPhone or iPad.

- **Outread.** This app is perhaps one of the most versatile of all speed reading apps. You can choose to download any eBook you own to the app, upload a Word document, pick a book from the app's extensive library, or read text from online pages by pasting URLs or linking to specific newsreader apps. Outread will present the text by either flashing one word at a time or by highlighting a word at a time from a fully visible text.

Additionally, a daytime and nighttime mode allows you to adjust the brightness of your screen to make reading more comfortable on your eyes. This app is compatible with iPhone or iPad devices.

- **Spreeder**. Perhaps one of the most comprehensive speed reading apps, Spreeder provides not only the tools needed for practicing speed reading, but it also provides access to reports that show your progress as well as guided training regimens. You can upload files to read, access books from your cloud library, or directly link to websites to create an unlimited selection of reading material. The basic app is free to use, but you can purchase an upgrade that will take your speed reading training to a whole new level. Spreeder is compatible with a whole range of devices, including iPhone, iPad, Mac, Web and Windows.

Conclusion

Now that you have read this book you have all the tools you need to develop your speed reading skills. By identifying and breaking your bad reading habits you can free yourself from all of the behaviors that have served to slow you down. Once your bad habits are gone you can replace them with those that will help you to increase your reading speed by three to four times. Finally, you can choose the speed reading techniques that are right for the style of reading that you do on a regular basis. Whether you read for pleasure, for work or just to stay caught up on current events, you can do so in a fraction of the time while gaining more information than ever before. The important thing is to practice every day, even if it's just for a few minutes. By practicing regularly you will develop your ability to read faster than ever, even getting to the place where you can read as much as a book a day!

www.ingramcontent.com/pod-product-compliance
Lightning Source LLC
LaVergne TN
LVHW010429070526
838199LV00066B/5970